ESCAPING A POW CAMP

BY JACQUE SUMMERS

E OF
ENTS

.........................4

EY...................7

......................13

......................19

P.......................25

ut It 29
ry 30
More 31
ography 31
32
uthor 32

FAST FACTS

- A prisoner of war (POW) is a person who has been captured by an enemy during a time of war. Enemy forces hold POWs in enclosed or remote areas, or camps.

- Since the Revolutionary War (1775–1783), more than 500,000 Americans have been captured and held as POWs.

- In some wars, such as the Revolutionary War, POWs were held captive on prison ships.

- In other wars, POW camps often consisted of buildings or enclosed, outdoor spaces. These camps were usually crowded. In many cases, POWs were mistreated. Some died from torture, starvation, or disease.

- In 1929, 47 countries signed a **treaty** in Geneva, Switzerland. The treaty set up laws about the treatment of POWs. The laws said that soldiers who are held captive during war should not be tortured, starved, or killed, and that they should receive medical treatment. But during World War II (1939–1945), countries such as Germany and Japan did not follow these laws.

er, 1; AP Images, 5; Philip Meeder/
Alexander Gardner/AP Images,
ves and Related Prints/Library
ion/Getty Images, 18; Nikolay
ges, 24, 26; iStockphoto, 28

POWs are held by enemy forces in enclosed or ▶ remote areas.

- In 1949, four additional treaties were signed to establish better protections for POWs and others affected in times of war.

Chapter 1

THE HMS *JERSEY*

Seventeen-year-old Christopher Hawkins gripped the handle of an axe. It was the fall of 1781. Christopher had been held captive aboard the HMS *Jersey*, a British prison ship, for only three days. But he was ready to make his escape.

Christopher and fellow American captive William Waterman waited in the semi-darkness belowdecks on the ship. They heard a clap of thunder. They immediately got to work. While the thunder boomed outside, they attacked the **gunport** with the axe and a crowbar. They had stolen these items from the upper deck of the ship. The thunder drowned out the clanging noise of metal against metal. After a while, the iron bars and bolts of the gunport came loose. The first part of their escape plan had succeeded. But at nightfall, they would have to brave the cold waters of Wallabout Bay. They would have to swim 2.5 miles (4.0 km) to the shore of Long Island, New York, while British guards patrolled the bay.

◄ **During the Revolutionary War, approximately 11,000 American POWs died aboard prison ships.**

Christopher had been captured by the British a few days earlier while sailing in the Atlantic Ocean. He had been a crew member aboard a ship led by Captain William Whipple. The crew's purpose was to capture or destroy British ships. America and Britain were at war. The 13 American **colonies**, which had been under British rule, wanted to be free from the British. Disagreements between the colonists and the British led to the Revolutionary War. Captain Whipple and Christopher took up the cause on the colonists' side.

Christopher joined Captain Whipple's crew in 1781. They sailed along the East Coast of North America. But after only five days at sea, British ships had surrounded them. Christopher and Captain Whipple were taken aboard a British ship and transferred to the HMS *Jersey*, one among a number of British prison ships anchored in Wallabout Bay.

Each night on the HMS *Jersey*, British soldiers herded the 800 prisoners belowdecks. The British did not feed them much food or water. Many POWs died from starvation or dehydration. Men moaned in pain. In the close quarters, diseases spread quickly.

Christopher quickly became friends with William Waterman. They came up with a plan to escape through the ship's gunport.

Today, Wallabout Bay is the site of the Brooklyn Navy Yard. ▶

MAJOR WARS AND POWS

War	Number of American POWs (Approximate)
Revolutionary War (1775–1783)	20,000
War of 1812 (1812–1815)	5,000
U.S. Civil War (1861–1865)	408,000
World War I (1914–1918)	4,120
World War II (1939–1945)	124,000
Korean War (1950–1953)	7,100
Vietnam War (1955–1975)	766

Other POWs had tried to escape from the deck of the ship. They had been quickly shot by British guards. But it would be more difficult for guards to see people escape from the gunport.

Christopher and William also hoped the darkness of night would hide them.

Christopher told Captain Whipple about the escape plan. But Captain Whipple did not come along. He did not think it would be possible for them to swim to the shore of Long Island in such cold waters.

On the night of their escape, Christopher and William collected what few clothes and little money they had. They wrapped their belongings in a bundle. Fellow prisoners lowered them down through the broken gunport by a bit of rope they had stolen. William climbed down first. Christopher followed.

The men aimed for the lights on the shore. The strong current tugged at them. Christopher lost sight of William. After two hours of swimming, Christopher could no longer hold onto his bundle. He let go of his belongings and watched them drift away. Finally, he made it to land and pulled himself ashore.

For a few days, Christopher wandered farther inland. Then he came across a barn. Farmers fed him bread and gave him new clothes. Other people he encountered on his journey also fed and sheltered him. One of the people Christopher met helped him find a ship. The ship brought him back home to his mother in Rhode Island. He later learned that his companion, William, had also successfully made it ashore.

Chapter 2

LIBBY PRISON

Thomas Rose peeked his head out of the underground passage. It was around 4:00 a.m. on February 9, 1864. For five long months, Thomas had been held captive in Libby Prison in Richmond, Virginia. But now, he had finally escaped.

Thomas was a Union soldier who had fought in the U.S. Civil War (1861–1865). The war started when the southern states attempted to separate from the northern states because of disagreements over slavery. The southern states formed the Confederacy. The northern states formed the Union. The Union fought to end slavery and keep the country united.

Since the start of the war, thousands of soldiers from both the Union and Confederate armies had been captured in battle. Many prison camps were needed on both sides to hold the captives. Thomas had been captured by enemy Confederate soldiers in September 1863. He had been fighting with the men of the 77th Pennsylvania **Infantry** in the Battle of Chickamauga.

◄ **The Confederate Army opened Libby Prison in 1861 to house Union POWs.**

▲ Today, monuments at the site of the Battle of Chickamauga honor the lives lost during the battle.

Over the course of two days, Union and Confederate soldiers had clashed along the banks of the Chickamauga Creek in Tennessee.

Nearly 4,000 soldiers were killed in the Battle of Chickamauga, making it the second-bloodiest battle in the Civil War. On the Union side, more than 1,600 soldiers were killed. More than 4,700 Union soldiers were captured or went missing.

Thomas was among the captured. He was brought to Libby Prison by train. Other captured Union soldiers were also packed onto the train. Onlookers lined the streets in Richmond as the southern soldiers marched the POWs to the prison. People spat and hissed at the POWs.

Libby Prison was a three-story warehouse that had been converted into a POW camp. Thomas was crammed in with 1,200 other Union soldiers. Prisoners were kept in six small rooms on the top two floors. Rice, cornbread, and small portions of meat were the only food provided. A layer of straw on the hard floor was their only bedding. The straw was never changed. It was filled with small insects, including lice and fleas. The small windows were covered with wooden bars. Sometimes the guards would tie and gag prisoners. They left men in those positions for hours.

Thomas found a friend in a fellow captive named Andrew Hamilton. Both men were determined to break out. They spent weeks studying the patterns of the guards. Guards were stationed throughout the prison. They guarded the prisoners every hour of the day. Guards were ordered to shoot any prisoner who approached a window. Thomas and Andrew learned that the only way out would be to dig a tunnel below the prison.

Thomas noticed that the kitchen on the lower floor of the building was not guarded at night. He explored the kitchen area. He discovered a hollow spot behind the kitchen stove.

Thomas and Andrew got to work. They removed bricks and dug a hole in the floor of the fireplace. The hole led to the cellar below.

Thomas, Andrew, and 13 other soldiers began digging in the cellar on October 1, 1863. They used a knife and other small tools they had stolen to dig. The men worked in complete darkness. Rats ran back and forth over their bodies.

The men sneaked down to the cellar each night to dig. After many nights, their tunnel was finally complete. Thomas crawled through the tunnel. The other men followed. At the end of the tunnel, they climbed out of a hole in groups of twos and threes.

It would be seven hours before the guards noticed anyone was missing. Thomas managed to evade capture for five days. He came within sight of the Union Army, but Confederate soldiers caught up to him in Williamsburg, Virginia. He was put back in Libby Prison and kept in **solitary confinement** for 30 days. He was fed only bread and water. Later, he was freed in a prisoner exchange. Thomas rejoined the Union Army and fought through the rest of the war.

◀ **Thomas joined the Union Army in 1861.**

Chapter 3

DAVAO PRISON

Twenty-seven-year-old Jack Hawkins peered through the thick jungle, hoping his wagon was still in place. Weeks of planning and gathering supplies had all come down to this. It was the morning of April 4, 1943. Jack and 11 other POWs were about to escape from Davao Prison.

Jack had been taken as a POW by Japanese soldiers during World War II. The United States joined the war in December 1941 after Japan attacked the U.S. naval base in Pearl Harbor, Hawaii. U.S. soldiers were sent to fight in two different areas: Europe and the Pacific. Jack had been transferred to the Philippines. He had fought in the Battle of Bataan, a four-month-long battle in early 1942 on Luzon Island in the Philippines. The battle ended with the Americans' surrender to the Japanese.

Japanese soldiers forced Jack and approximately 75,000 other American and Filipino soldiers on an eight-day march north. Their captors forced them to walk all day long in scorching heat.

◄ **Filipino and American prisoners were held captive at Davao Prison in the Philippines.**

▲ A memorial in Bataan, the Philippines,
honors U.S. and Filipino soldiers who
died in the Bataan Death March.

The POWs were forced to march for 65 miles (105 km). They were starved. Prisoners who couldn't keep up were whipped. During the march, approximately 3,000 POWs died from starvation, dehydration, or torture. This march is known as the Bataan Death March.

Once the survivors reached the town of San Fernando, their captors packed them into hot train cars. The train traveled north.

They reached the town of Capas. From there, Jack and a few hundred other POWs were later transported by ship to Davao Prison in the southern Philippines.

At Davao, POWs were tortured, starved, and forced to work on fields in the nearby **plantation**. Miles of thick jungle surrounded the fenced-in plantation. Jack and his companions endured these conditions for ten months while they plotted their escape. They managed to save morsels of food. They stole, traded, or bribed guards for materials. These included medicine, a compass, and a few knives. They managed to steal chickens, eggs, and onions.

FEMALE POWS

Many women were taken as POWs during World War II. They were nuns, doctors, teachers, and nurses. In May 1943, a group of nurses was captured and sent to a prison camp in Manilla, the capital of the Philippines. Later, when there were too many prisoners in that camp, some were moved to a camp near the town of Los Baños. The female POWs set up a hospital and took care of the sick with the few medicines and supplies that were available to them. They were freed in February 1945.

The POWs packed their supplies into a wagon, which they hid nearby in the jungle.

Their day of escape had finally come. Jack and the others told the guards that they needed to do extra work on the plantation. They walked out of the gates and toward their assigned fields. As soon as they were out of sight, they ran to their wagon.

They waded in knee-deep water for 20 miles (32 km) through a dark swamp. The swamp was filled with **leeches**, crocodiles, and razor-sharp grass that cut their skin. Walking through the swamp ooze was like walking through tar. They were attacked by mosquitoes and other bugs.

After three days, they realized that they were lost. They were about to give up when they heard gunfire. Japanese and Filipino soldiers were fighting nearby.

The POWs found the Filipino soldiers the next morning. The soldiers helped the POWs move from village to village. At long last, Jack boarded a U.S. military submarine in November 1943. The submarine took him and other Americans to Australia. Jack had endured a brutal march and months of mistreatment in a POW camp. But he was finally safe.

The Philippine islands are covered in miles of thick jungle. ▶

Chapter 4

TRAI BAI CAMP

On the night of July 8, 1965, Isaac "Ike" Camacho squinted through the heavy rain at the guard post outside the cage. He couldn't be sure that the guard was in the building, but he didn't want to delay his escape any longer. He bunched up his pajamas and arranged them on his cot. He hoped his Vietnamese captors would mistake the clothing for his sleeping body, at least until he was a safe distance from the camp. Then, he pulled aside a loose wooden bar in the cage and slid out into the dark and damp night.

Ike, a Mexican-American soldier from Texas, had been captured by Vietnamese forces while fighting in the Vietnam War (1954–1975). The war had started because North Vietnam had wanted the entire country to be under **communist** rule, but both South Vietnam and the United States opposed communism. The United States sent soldiers, including Ike, to South Vietnam. The U.S. troops joined the South Vietnamese in their fight against the North Vietnamese army, the Viet Cong.

◄ **During the Vietnam War, some American POWs were kept in cages in North Vietnamese prison camps.**

▲ **In some North Vietnamese camps, POWs were contained by walls or barbed wire.**

On November 22, 1963, the Viet Cong attacked the U.S. camp of Hiêp Hòa in South Vietnam. Ike had been stationed at the camp. The Viet Cong captured Ike and other U.S. soldiers during the attack.

Viet Cong soldiers marched Ike and other American POWs south to Trai Bai, a small camp near the Cambodian border. Here, Ike was held in a small, wooden cage. His captors forced chains onto his feet. They fed the POWs salted rice and dried fish.

The fish was crawling with worms. In the daytime, Ike was forced to collect wood or do other manual labor. At night, bombs from U.S. forces sometimes exploded in the jungle nearby. Ike would scramble into a hole in the back of his cage, which served as a bomb shelter.

Ike was often sick from lack of nutrition. He lost a lot of weight. But he never lost hope that he would one day escape.

In early July 1965, the Viet Cong prepared to bring more POWs into camp. They built new cages. They took the chains off of Ike and other prisoners so they could use the chains on the newcomers.

JOHN McCAIN

Arizona senator John McCain was a POW during the Vietnam War. On October 26, 1967, his fighter plane was shot down over the city of Hanoi in North Vietnam. He escaped the crash, but his leg was so mangled that he could barely move. He spent nearly six years in Hỏa Lò Prison, a camp that was nicknamed the Hanoi Hilton. He was tortured and starved. When the United States signed a peace agreement with the North Vietnamese, American POWs were released. On March 14, 1973, John got on a plane and went home.

▲ **During monsoon season in Vietnam, it may rain for several days in a row.**

One day, Ike managed to pry a bar loose in his cage. Then he waited for nightfall.

Ike knew the best time to escape was **monsoon** season, when the heavy rain would wash away his tracks. On the night of July 8, Ike slipped from his cage and ran into the jungle. He jumped into the fast-flowing Saigon River. The strong current tugged at him. It carried him away from the camp.

Mosquitoes swarmed Ike day and night. When he emerged from the water, his body was covered in slimy leeches. But he found abundant fruit, such as mangoes and kiwis, growing in the jungle.

After four days, Ike spotted an American plane. He followed it. He came to a road and saw a motorbike with a red cross on it. The cross was a symbol used by medical volunteers. The driver took Ike to the U.S. Special Forces camp at Minh Tranh, South Vietnam. Ike received a hot shower, a new uniform, and food. After 20 months as a POW, Ike returned home to the United States. He received a hero's welcome.

THINK ABOUT IT

- Some prisoners felt it was better to risk death and attempt to escape rather than stay in a POW camp. Why do you think they were willing to take that risk?
- What do you think would be the hardest part of planning an escape from a POW camp?
- People who survive POW camps often return home. How might life for a POW camp survivor be different after such an experience?

GLOSSARY

colonies (KAH-luh-neez): Colonies are territories that are ruled by people from another country. The 13 American colonies wanted to separate from British rule, which led to the Revolutionary War.

communist (KAHM-yuh-nist): A communist is someone who believes in a system of government in which people share property and goods. North Vietnam was a communist country.

gunport (GUHN-port): A gunport is an opening on the side of a ship through which a gun can be fired. Christopher Hawkins and William Waterman escaped the HMS *Jersey* prison ship through a gunport.

infantry (IN-fuhn-tree): An infantry is a group of trained soldiers. Thomas Rose was part of the 77th Pennsylvania Infantry.

leeches (LEECH-iz): Leeches are types of worms that live in water and that survive by sucking on the blood of animals. Jack Hawkins and his companions waded in water filled with leeches.

monsoon (mahn-SOON): A monsoon is a weather event that causes heavy rainfall during the summer in South Asia. The heavy rains during the monsoon season washed away Ike Camacho's footprints.

plantation (plan-TAY-shuhn): A plantation is a large farm where crops are grown and harvested. At Davao Prison, POWs were forced to work on a plantation.

solitary confinement (SAHL-uh-tair-ee kuhn-FINE-muhnt): Solitary confinement is a punishment in which a person is put in complete isolation. After he was recaptured by Confederate soldiers, Thomas Rose was put in solitary confinement in Libby Prison.

treaty (TREE-tee): A treaty is a written agreement between two or more countries. A 1929 treaty signed by world leaders in Geneva, Switzerland, established protections for POWs.

TO LEARN MORE

Books

Adams, Simon. *World War I*. New York, NY: DK Publishing, 2014.

Figley, Marty Rhodes. *The Prison-Ship Adventure of James Forten, Revolutionary War Captive*. Minneapolis, MN: Graphic Universe, 2011.

Streissguth, Tom. *The Vietnam War*. Mankato, MN: The Child's World, 2015.

Web Sites

Visit our Web site for links about escaping a POW camp: childsworld.com/links

Note to Parents, Teachers, and Librarians: We routinely verify our Web links to make sure they are safe and active sites. So encourage your readers to check them out!

SELECTED BIBLIOGRAPHY

Burrows, Edwin G. *Forgotten Patriots: The Untold Story of American Prisoners during the Revolutionary War*. New York, NY: Basic Books, 2008.

Lukacs, John D. *Escape from Davao: The Forgotten Story of the Most Daring Prison Break of the Pacific War*. New York, NY: Simon & Schuster, 2010.

Wheelan, Joseph. *Libby Prison Breakout: The Daring Escape from the Notorious Civil War Prison*. New York, NY: PublicAffairs, 2010.

INDEX

Bataan Death March, 20

Camacho, Isaac, 25–29

Civil War, 10, 13–14

Davao Prison, 19, 21–22

Hamilton, Andrew, 15

Hawkins, Christopher, 7–8, 10–11

Hawkins, Jack, 19–22

HMS *Jersey*, 7–8, 10–11

Libby Prison, 13–15, 17

McCain, John, 27

prison ships, 4, 7–8, 10–11

Revolutionary War, 4, 8, 10

Rose, Thomas, 13–15, 17

Trai Bai, 25–29

treaties, 4–5

Vietnam War, 10, 25–26

Waterman, William, 7, 8, 10–11

World War II, 4, 10, 19, 21

ABOUT THE AUTHOR

Jacque Summers has a degree in creative writing. She is passionate about history, science, nature, and society. She is the author of two nonfiction books. She lives with her husband, who is a history teacher, and their four children in central California.